PAGES FROM
MY LIFE'S BOOK

Books by Derek Prince

Biography
Appointment in Jerusalem
Pages from My Life's Book

Guides to the Life of Faith
Atonement: Your Appointment with God
Baptism in the Holy Spirit
Blessing or Curse: You Can Choose
The Divine Exchange
Does Your Tongue Need Healing?
Extravagant Love
Faith to Live By
Fasting
Fatherhood
God Is a Matchmaker
God's Medicine Bottle
God's Plan for Your Money
God's Remedy for Rejection
The Grace of Yielding
The Holy Spirit in You
How to Fast Successfully
Husbands and Fathers

Judging: When? Why? How?
Life's Bitter Pool
The Marriage Covenant
Objective for Living: To Do God's Will
Prayers and Proclamations
Promised Land
Protection from Deception
Receiving God's Best
Shaping History Through Prayer & Fasting
Spiritual Warfare
Surviving the Last Days
They Shall Expel Demons
Through the Psalms
War in Heaven
Who Is the Holy Spirit?

Systematic Bible Exposition
Prophetic Destinies
Self Study Bible Course
The Spirit-filled Believer's Handbook

DEREK PRINCE

PAGES FROM MY LIFE'S BOOK

Derek Prince Ministries–International
Charlotte, North Carolina U.S.A.

PAGES FROM MY LIFE'S BOOK

Copyright © 1987 Derek Prince Ministries–International

Published by Derek Prince Ministries–International 2005

ISBN 978-1-892283-14-6

This book is an edited transcript of *Pages From My Life's Book* from the *Keys to Successful Living* daily radio program.

Cover by Ronna Fu.

Printed in the United States of America.

Derek Prince Ministries–International
http://www.derekprince.org

CONTENTS

PART I

SEARCH FOR TRUTH

1
THE IMPORTANCE OF
PERSONAL TESTIMONY

The personal experiences in my walk with God have built my faith and shaped my life's destiny. I will begin with my personal search for truth as a young man.

Before I relate any personal experiences, I would like to establish one basic principle of Scripture: God expects us, as Christians, to share our personal testimony with those around us. Acts 1:8 is the final words of Jesus spoken to His disciples as He was standing with them on the Mount of Olives, before He was taken up again to heaven. I always feel there is a special significance in the last words a man speaks to those who have been very close to him, knowing that he is not going to meet them again the same way. Because of this, I have always attached great importance to these final words of Jesus:

> ". . . but you shall receive power when the Holy Spirit has come upon you; and you shall be My witnesses both in Jerusalem,

and in all Judea and Samaria, and even to
the remotest part of the earth."

(NAS)

It is significant, I believe, that the last words that fell
from the lips of Jesus on earth were, "the remotest part of
the earth." I believe Jesus had in mind that this testimony of
Him and His gospel should be carried to every nation, every
people, every tribe, every tongue, all races everywhere,
everyone who lives on the face of the earth. His mind was
fixed on this as He left His disciples, and He gave a very
simple, two-stage process by which this task could be
carried out. First, every believer needs to be personally
empowered by the Holy Spirit. This is very practical. The
message that we must carry as Christians is a supernatural
message. It centers in supernatural events—the death and
resurrection of Jesus—and it needs a supernatural power to
make it real and vivid to those to whom we speak. The
supernatural power that God has ordained and made
available is the power of the Holy Spirit.

The second step is that each believer tells others what
God has done for him or her. This process is perpetual. Each
believer who hears and believes, is in turn empowered by
the Holy Spirit and tells others; those others, in turn, as they
believe, are empowered by the Holy Spirit and go on to tell
others. In this way, if we are faithful, the testimony of Jesus
and the message of the Gospel can indeed be carried to "the
remotest part of the earth."

We must make a very important distinction between
witnessing and preaching. Preaching is proclaiming the
truth of Scripture. It is a ministry God gives particularly to
some of His servants. Witnessing, however, is different.

Witnessing is talking in a personal way about our own experience. It is telling others what God has done in our lives. Even though not all Christians are called to preach, all true Christians should be witnesses.

Notice that Jesus does not say, "You will witness," He says, "You will *be* witnesses." In other words, it is not just our words, but it is the life we live that must testify to Jesus and what He has done in our lives. Sometimes, if people do not live the life, it is better for them not to talk too much about it! Jesus' program is that each one of us should be a witness wherever we are: in the home, in the workplace, in the school, or in the university. Wherever it may be, Jesus wants us to be His witnesses, both to talk and live in such a way that we reflect what Jesus has done in our lives.

It is a remarkable fact that the Christian faith conquered the Roman Empire within three centuries. The Roman Empire was undoubtedly one of the most powerful, proud, and long-lived empires in human history. It was regarded in its day as the very epitome of power and authority. Yet, in less than three centuries from the time that Jesus spoke those words on the Mount of Olives to that little group of men, the Roman emperor himself had bowed the knee at the name of Jesus—the name of a Jewish carpenter's son—who had been crucified on a Roman cross by a Roman governor. It was almost inconceivable that such a thing could happen, yet Christianity had conquered the Roman Empire. How? Not by revolution, not by war, not by staging marches or making protests, but by spiritual weapons.

Perhaps the most universal and effective of all those spiritual weapons was the testimony of the early Christians. They came from many different backgrounds, different races, different religions, different social levels. They had just one thing in common: they had met Jesus and He had changed their lives. The whole ancient world could not stand up against the impact of their testimony.

In Ephesians 3:10, we read this about God's purpose for the church. His intent was that now, through the church, "the manifold wisdom of God might now be made known . . . to the rulers and the authorities in the heavenly places." It is through the church that God is going to demonstrate His manifold, many-sided wisdom to the universe.

The wisdom of God is like a diamond, cut with many facets, and each believer is just one facet. Each believer has some unique aspect of God's wisdom to reveal to the world and he reveals it by his testimony.

In connection with the importance of personal testimony, I want to point out the primary responsibility for which apostles were chosen and appointed by God. After the disloyalty and suicide of Judas, it became necessary for another man to be appointed an apostle in his place. Peter spoke to the believers gathered and told them why it was necessary and what kind of man should be chosen to take the place of Judas. This is what Peter said in Acts 1:21–22:

> "Therefore it is necessary to choose one of the men who have been with us the whole time the Lord Jesus went in and out among us, beginning from John's baptism to the time when Jesus was taken up from us. For one of these must become a witness with us of his resurrection." (NIV)

There are two key words here: "witness" and "resurrection." The primary function of an apostle was not to be a preacher or a teacher, that was secondary. The primary function of an apostle was to be a witness of what he himself had seen and heard of Jesus. Those original apostles had to be witnesses of the life and ministry of Jesus from the time of John's baptism to the time of Jesus' death and resurrection. There was one particular thing to which they had to give testimony, the most important thing of all: His resurrection. The resurrection is the central fact of the Christian faith. It is the good news that the whole world needs to hear.

I am reminded of the words of a hymn that I particularly love, which ends with these words: "May the Book of Life never close 'til the whole world knows; He arose, He arose." That is my prayer, that the Book of Life may not close until every human being on the face of the earth has heard this one vital fact of human history: that death has been conquered and that Jesus arose. This is a life-changing fact, a fact that can bring hope and peace where there is despair and loneliness and utter hopelessness.

Let us look at the words spoken to Paul, the apostle-to-be, when he was still Saul of Tarsus. In the city of Damascus, God sent Ananias to pray for Saul of Tarsus that he might receive his sight. This is Paul's own testimony of what Ananias said to him, given in Acts 22:14–15:

> "Then he [Ananias] said: 'The God of our fathers has chosen you [Paul] to know his will and to see the Righteous One and to hear words from his mouth. You will be his witness to all men of what you have seen and heard.' " (NIV)

Again, notice the primary calling in the life of Paul. He was not to be a preacher; he was primarily called to be a witness to all men of what he had seen and heard. A witness is a person who speaks firsthand of what he has seen and heard.

Then we read Paul's words in Acts 26:22–23, where he gave a defense of himself before King Agrippa:

> "But I have had God's help to this very day, and so I stand here and testify to small and great alike. I am saying nothing beyond what the prophets and Moses said would happen—that the Christ would suffer and, as the first to rise from the dead, would proclaim light to his own people and to the Gentiles." (NIV)

Paul was testifying to everybody, small and great, no one too high or too low. His testimony was directed toward two sources of his personal experience: first, Moses and the prophets (the Scriptures); secondly, the death and resurrection of Jesus Christ. Our testimony should do the same.

2
SEARCHING IN
PHILOSOPHY

I was born in India of British parents during World War I. My entire family background was military. I have never met a male relative in my family who was not an officer in the British Army. I am the only existing exception to that rule.

As soon as the war ended, my family sent me home to Britain for the benefit of my health and my education. Education became the major factor in my life for the next twenty years. At the age of nine, I was sent away to a boarding school and from nine to twenty-five I spent most of each year in various boarding schools, colleges or universities.

At thirteen, I was successful in a competitive examination for boys of that age all over Britain (the cream of Britain's intellectual upper class), and I was admitted as a scholar to Eton College, which is Britain's oldest, largest, most expensive, most exclusive, and probably most snobbish boarding school for boys. When I was eighteen, I was again successful in an examination and was awarded a scholarship to King's College in the University of Cambridge. My main education was in the Greek and Roman Classics.

I can remember starting to learn Latin when I was nine years old and Greek when I was ten. By the age of thirteen, I was expected to be able to write verse in both Latin and Greek.

My religious background was in the Anglican Church, which is the English state church. I really knew no other church. During my school years, we were compelled to attend church once every weekday and twice on Sunday – eight times a week.

As I looked around at the people in the church, I gradually became disillusioned. When I reached my teens, I had the typical teenage tendency of being critical and rebellious, mistrustful of authority and the older generation. I always remember that every Sunday morning in the Anglican Church we were led in a certain prayer. In this prayer we repeated, "Pardon us, miserable offenders." By the time I was about thirteen or fourteen years old, I would look around at those people saying, "Pardon us, miserable offenders," and I would say to myself, "They surely are miserable." There was no doubt in my mind that I, too, was an offender. I was doing all sorts of things I knew I should not be doing. Then I came to this conclusion: I could be an offender without religion and not be nearly so miserable. So that was my secret determination.

As long as I remained at Eton I had no choice; I was required to go to chapel once every weekday and twice every Sunday. In my mind I reflected: Christianity is a harmless occupation for old ladies of both sexes!

Another way I described Christianity was: A crutch with which weak-minded people hobble through life. But I was not weak-minded, I did not need the crutch, and I was going to throw it away just as soon as I could.

When I got to Cambridge University, church-going was no longer compulsory, and I took that crutch of Christianity and I threw it away from me as far as I could throw it. However, there remained inside me a gnawing realization that somewhere there must be a meaning and a purpose to life. Christianity as I knew it had failed to provide the answer. It must be somewhere. Where could I look?

I decided that philosophy had the answer, so I became a student of philosophy. The philosophy I studied most was that of Plato, who is undoubtedly one of the outstanding intellects of human history. I was able to read Plato in the original Greek and I read every word that he ever wrote in that language. I combined my study of ancient philosophy with various forms of modern philosophy.

The form of philosophy that was fashionable in those days was known as Logical Positivism. It centered around finding the right meaning of words. Its thesis was that if you really understood what words meant, you would not bother about being a philosopher. It was a strange, mixed-up kind of occupation. I remember that we spent one whole term in the philosophy class at Cambridge discussing whether we could know that the desk from which the professor lectured was really there. As a matter of fact, as far as I remember, we never did resolve that problem. In a way, philosophy, too, was somewhat confusing.

I was intellectually gifted; I have always been at home in the world of words, definitions and theories. I was always the most successful student at the university in my particular field. For two years I held the Senior University Research Studentship in Philosophy, which is a distinction that few people have ever enjoyed. This is not to boast, but to indicate that a lack of intellect was not the source of my frustration.

Finding that philosophy did not have a very clear or positive answer, I turned to Oriental cults and systems such as are extremely fashionable in our contemporary society. I was probably about one generation ahead of many of these people, though I did not realize it. I turned to Yoga, to Theosophy, and even to Voodoo. When I look back, I either smile or laugh at my simplicity. To the best of my ability, I became a practicing yogi. I practiced meditational and positional yoga. But again, I ended up in disillusionment. I had a certain kind of supernatural experience, but it did not make me happy. In fact, it was followed by a grey depression that settled around me.

My problem was that I was in many ways an idealist. When I studied Plato, I could see his ideal picture of the ideal city, the ideal state, the ideal laws, and the ideal government. It really appealed to me, but I always came back to earth with a bump! I was not in the ideal. I was confronted with the actual, not only in other people but, worst of all, in myself. The actual, both in other people and in myself, was so far from the ideal that it was intensely frustrating. I could discover no way to bridge the gap between the ideal and the actual.

One result of all this was that I developed chronic indigestion. I was carefully examined in one of the best hospitals in Britain with all sorts of x-rays and tests, but there seemed to be no diagnosable cause for my indigestion and, therefore, no cure. I believe it was really an emotional reaction to the frustration experienced when I contemplated the ideal and saw how far away the actual was from the ideal.

The only relief I could discover from the pressure and indigestion was whiskey. Whiskey had always been an accepted drink in my parents' home. Nobody felt any reproach about whiskey. I remember as a boy of sixteen I surreptitiously sneaked a little whiskey when nobody was looking, put it in a glass, and splashed some soda into it. I drank it and immediately felt about two inches taller. By the time I had reached my twenties, however, it took a bottle of whiskey to do the same for me that that little splash in a glass had done some years earlier.

When I could not stand the tension between the ideal and the actual any longer, a friend and I would listen to classical music and drink whiskey. When we had finished one bottle, we would often go on to the second. I had one particular friend who was quite expert in music. In those days, there were no stereo systems and, in order to get the best reproduction, you needed a curving, nine-foot horn attached to your gramophone or phonograph. We would sit there with this horn sticking out over our heads, giving out this glorious music, and drinking our whiskey. We would look at one another and wonder whether we had the solution to life or not.

Looking back, I can say about that period in my life that I achieved academic success. I was one of the youngest persons ever to be elected to a Fellowship at King's College, Cambridge. Those words probably do not mean much in the United States, but in Britain that is a very high academic distinction. I became a kind of resident professor and a member of the governing body of my college. I had achieved success; I had a certain reputation. I had written a dissertation of Plato's method of definition and its evolution. I knew a lot of long words and phrases and had tried a lot of different things. But, looking back, I would have to admit I was confused and frustrated, disappointed and disillusioned, and did not know where to find the answer.

3
THE ARMY AND
THE BIBLE

At this stage in my life, World War II broke out and plunged the whole continent of Europe into upheaval and confusion. Mine was one of millions of lives that was permanently changed by the impact of that war. I realized that I was going to be drafted into the British Army. For years I wondered what I would do when this situation came. I had always thought that the right thing to do would be to take the stand of a conscientious objector. Because of my family background, however, that was a very difficult decision. It was not that I based my conclusions on Christianity, rather I based them on philosophy.

Eventually, I took the stand of a conscientious objector and went before a tribunal. My objections were accepted as valid and I was drafted into the Army Medical Corps as a hospital attendant, with a guarantee that I would never be required to use military weapons.

I was at the end of a stage in my life, about to leave Cambridge University and go into a totally different type of life and an unknown future. The thing that troubled me most was that I would be required to leave the libraries behind. Up to that time, I had had some of the largest and best-stocked libraries in Europe available to me any time I wanted to consult a book. Now I was going into the British Army and I knew that I would be required to carry all my worldly possessions in a long, black bag (which in the Army is called a "kit bag") and that books are heavy. I did not want to drag a lot of books around with me, yet I had to have something to read.

At that point, I reasoned with myself in a philosophic sort of way and said, "There is one book that is more widely read and more influential than any other book in human history. It is a book of philosophy and I really don't know much about it. I ought to study it." You know the book that I had in mind? The Bible. I am glad that, even in those days, I had enough sense to recognize the unique significance of the Bible in human history.

Undoubtedly, the Bible is what I termed it: The most widely read and influential book in the history of the human race. So I determined it was my philosophic duty to take a Bible with me and read it. I bought a nice, new, black Bible and went into the British Army with it.

I did not realize, of course, that when a person reads the Bible in the army he becomes extremely conspicuous. I will always remember my first night in the barrack room with about twenty-four other new enlisted soldiers. I sat down on the bed, opened my Bible, and started to read it. I asked myself, "Where do you start any book?" The answer, "At the first chapter."

So I began in Genesis, chapter one, verse one. As soon as the other soldiers saw me reading my Bible, however, a kind of uneasy hush fell on the whole room and everybody began to look my way.

It was an extraordinary thing, though—when I was not reading the Bible, I was living a life that was very unlike that which is led by most people who read the Bible. I am ashamed when I look back, but I had become a very heavy drinker of whiskey. I was not an alcoholic, but whenever I was frustrated I would turn to whiskey for release, and the only release I got was to drink too much.

Worse still, I was an habitual blasphemer. With deep regret and shame I confess that I continually used unclean and blasphemous words. It was bad when I entered the army, and after six months in the army I was awful. Basically, the British Army has probably the most blasphemous group of men found anywhere in humanity. I was every bit as bad as the rest.

There I was, reading my Bible, drinking my whiskey, blaspheming—baffling everybody and feeling baffled myself. The Bible baffled me. It was the first book I had read that I did not understand. I could not classify it. Was it history? Was it mythology? Was it poetry? Was it philosophy? It did not seem to fit into any of those categories. I also found it very hard going and very boring, but I was a determined person and I said to myself, "No book is going to beat me. I've started to read this book, and I'm going to read it through from beginning to end."

Every day I sat down and read something out of the Bible. In fact, I read it in consecutive order, starting at Genesis, chapter one, verse one, and I went on through it.

At the end of about nine months in the army, I had reached the book of Job, and then something happened that had a transforming impact on the rest of my life.

My company was transferred to another area of England, to the county of Yorkshire, which is in the north of England. I had always grown up in the south of England, so I discovered that the people in Yorkshire were unusually friendly and hospitable, often inviting soldiers into their homes for meals. I was invited into the home of a Christian family, but they were not the kind of Christians that I had known previously. First of all, they were very humble, uneducated people. But there was something different about them. I could not identify it, but I felt it the moment I walked into their home.

They invited me for a meal so we sat around their table, and the first thing they did was pray over the meal. I had never been in a home where anybody prayed over the food, but I adjusted to that and enjoyed the meal. Then at the end of the meal, without any warning, they started to pray again. There were about seven or eight people around a big, oval table and I realized to my horror that they were praying in turn and that my turn was coming, and quickly!

I had never prayed out loud in public all my life. I had no idea what to say or do. It would be no exaggeration to say that panic gripped me. When my turn came, I opened my mouth and blurted out these words: "Lord, I believe; help Thou my unbelief." After I said that, my mouth shut like a trap and I could say no more. I thought to myself, "Where did I get those words from? How could I ever say anything like that?"

In particular, I was interested in the lady of the home. She was a little, frail woman, in about her late fifties, who had obviously had a pretty hard life. She told me something that absolutely shook me. In World War I her husband had been exempted from military service because it was discovered that he had tuberculosis of one lung. I knew that for him to gain military exemption, it had to be a valid medical diagnosis. Then she said to me, "I prayed for my husband every day for ten years."

I thought to myself, "Could anybody pray about anything every day for ten years?" I could not conceive a person doing anything like that.

But what she went on to say was even more astonishing. "At the end of ten years," she said, "I was praying alone in a room. My husband was in the bedroom, sitting up in bed, propped up on the pillows, coughing up blood. As I was praying, an audible voice spoke to me and said, 'Claim it!' I answered out loud, 'Lord, I claim it now!'"

When she said that, her husband, in the bed in the other room, was healed of tuberculosis. When he went back to the doctor to be examined, the doctor told him that the lung that had been affected was stronger than the lung that had never been affected!

They were very simple, uneducated people. They were probably incapable of any kind of guile or superficiality. Consequently, when I heard how this woman had prayed for ten years and her husband had been healed of tuberculosis, something in me asked, "Is this what you've been looking for?"

I thought to myself, "Maybe it is!"

But I just could not understand the kind of language that these people used. I could honestly say, if they had spoken Greek, I would have understood them better. They could not communicate to me what it was they had nor how they got it.

4
MEETING JESUS

Being with that Christian family in Yorkshire, I realized two things: first, for them the Bible was a meaningful, up-to-date book; and second, they had a real, personal relationship with God. I felt cheated that after so many years at Britain's largest university, I could not understand the Bible and they could. I asked myself, "Is this what I've been looking for?" But when I asked that question, three other questions immediately came to my mind. I began to think about the implications of getting involved in whatever it was that these people had and I saw that it was something that took up their whole lives.

The three questions were:

If I get involved in this, what will happen to my university career?

What will my friends say?

Finally, worst of all, what will my family say? It was a disgrace when I became a conscientious objector, but suppose I become a religious fanatic on top of that?

These questions bombarded my mind, and I walked around for a time almost unconscious of my surroundings. I was going through a deep, internal conflict between the desire for what these people had and fear as to the consequences of getting involved in it. I continually said to myself, "Well, what about my career? What about my friends? What about my family?"

After four or five days of this, I reached a decisive point. I summed it up this way: I don't care what happens to my career. I don't care what my friends say. I don't care what my family says. I want this thing, whatever it is. I don't understand what it is, but whatever it is, I want it.

When I made that decision I thought, "Well, how do I get it?"

The only thing I could think of was to pray. One evening, quite late, I went back to the army barrack rooms which I shared with one other soldier. I determined to pray until something happened.

We had no beds at that time; we slept on straw mattresses on the floor. I waited until the other soldier was asleep on his mattress, then placed a little folding canvas stool which I had in front of the window. I sat on the stool, placed my elbows on the windowsill and decided to pray. But once more I was baffled.

I realized that I had no idea how to pray. I did not know to whom I should pray or what I should say. I just could not even begin.

I suppose I sat there on that stool for one hour or more as darkness descended, trying to pray. But once again, I was totally baffled.

Then something happened that I find hard to explain. Just when I was ready to give up, an unknown power contacted me and made itself real to me. When I say a "power," I am referring to something that was extremely powerful. The first thing that happened was my arms began to go up in the air, and as they went up I noticed the palms were upwards, towards the ceiling. I asked myself, "Why with the palms upward?"

Something within me answered, "It is power from on high."

I realized by a sudden revelation that I had previously been in touch with a power from below but never up to this time had I made contact with power from on high.

In the moving of this power upon me, I became aware of a person. It was as though, through the power, a person was coming to me. I did not know who the person was, but I knew that this was the person who had the answer for me. Words began to come out of my mouth that I did not choose. I began to say, "Unless you bless me, I will not let you go!" When I got to those words, "I will not let you go!" something took over and I could not stop saying them. "I will not let you go! I will not let you go! I will not let you go!"

This mysterious power that was moving my arms upwards took my whole body, lifted me off that stool, and deposited me on the floor with my arms still in the air and still saying, "I will not let you go! I will not let you go, unless you bless me!" Somehow I knew that I had met a Person for the first time whom I had never met and never known before; the Person who was the answer to my searching.

As I lay there on the floor with my arms in the air, speaking to this unknown person for the first time in my life, the power seemed to flow over me like a sea. I seemed to be submerged beneath a mysterious, invisible, but very real, power. It was going over me like waves of the sea.

Then something broke loose in the innermost part of my being. It was as though there was a release, like a knot that had been tied there for many years had been undone.

This power now began to flow out of my body like a river, carrying all sorts of debris and unclean things before it. I pictured a river in a flood that had broken loose and was carrying everything before it. It was as though unknown, evil forces were being flushed out of my body by this strange, mysterious river of power. I was fearful. I really did not know where I was being carried or what was going to happen next. Yet I kept saying to myself, "You've got this far. If you try to stop now, you may never get this far again."

Strange things happened inside me. I began to sob, and tears flowed out of me. I had no idea why I was sobbing. I had no consciousness in my mind of anything about which I needed to cry, but still the tears flowed out of me. That was strange enough, but after about an hour of this, the tears began to change to laughter. Again, I had no conscious reason to be laughing. In fact, it was not really I who was laughing. Laughter was just flowing out through me and I felt myself submerging in this sea of laughter.

Over the top of my head, I saw the blanket move as the other soldier began to awaken. He gradually emerged from under the blanket wearing only his underclothes. He got to his feet and rather slowly and reluctantly walked towards me. He walked around me two or three times and said, "I don't know what to do with you! I suppose it's no good throwing water over you."

I could not answer him but something inside me said, "Even water wouldn't put this out!"

Then another strange thing happened. Words came to me, I do not know from where, that "A man must not blaspheme against the Holy Spirit." Contrary to all my reasoning, I knew that the Holy Spirit was in me, so I decided that I would not allow my friend to say anything wrong. With great difficulty, I got to my knees, crawled to my mattress, took my place on it, drew the blanket up over me and lay there. But this laughter was still flowing through me.

In that way I came to know that Truth is a Person. I had always been looking for an abstraction, a theory. I had been looking for an explanation but had found a Person. Without any process of reasoning, I knew that that person was Jesus of Nazareth.

From that day to this, I have never doubted that Jesus is alive. I discovered what I had failed to understand for so long, that truth is not just an abstraction, religion or creed. Rather, it is a person. In Jesus, I finally resolved that awful conflict that had troubled me for so many years between the ideal and the actual. In Jesus, I discovered that the ideal is the actual. His life, words, and teaching, but above all, His person—they were the answer to that unsatisfied craving that had driven me for so many years.

5
RESULTS OF
MEETING JESUS

Tremendous changes immediately took place in my life as a result of meeting Jesus. I would like to describe these changes in an objective way, as far as possible.

First, I have never been able to doubt since that time that Jesus is alive. I might be tempted to disobey Him or be disloyal to Him, but I absolutely cannot doubt that Jesus is alive. From that moment until now, this has been the most important single fact in my life: that Jesus of Nazareth, the One who hung on a cross, was buried in a stone tomb and rose from the dead, is alive, and I know Him. This is not the result of reasoning. It is not the result of study. It is not the result of ministerial training. It is the result of an encounter. I met Him; He met me. I know Him. Every day I know Him. Every hour I am conscious of His presence.

Second, prayer became as natural to me as breathing. The night I tried to pray, I did not know how to pray, what words to say, or to whom to pray. The next day, as I went about my ordinary military duties, I discovered that I was praying all the time. I made no effort, instead each breath was a prayer. I remember going to a tap to draw some water to drink. Normally, that would have been a very ordinary thing to do and I would have attached no importance to it, but I just could not drink that water until I had thanked God for it. It seemed so natural to talk to God and thank Him.

I had always thought of prayer as something that you had to do in a religious building and in a religious type of attitude. I now discovered that prayer is communicating with God, and since the Holy Spirit came into me it was easy and natural for me to communicate with God. This communication with God gave me a source of inner strength. No matter what was going on around me, I had an inner communication with God which continued all the time I was awake.

Third, the Bible suddenly became a meaningful book. I had been reading it for nine months trying to make sense of it. I had read from the beginning of Genesis to the middle of the book of Job. I had made quite a lot of progress as far as reading was concerned but I could not classify the book or understand it. After I met Jesus and the Holy Spirit had come into my life, there was a total, immediate change in my relationship to the Bible. This was not gradual, nor was it the result of a process. It did not come from an intellectual struggle, but it came from this new relationship. I remember that I had decided I would go on reading where I had stopped, in the middle of Job. I turned the pages of my Bible and happened to open, without seeking it, to Psalm 126, and read the first two verses:

> When the Lord turned again the captivity of
> Zion, we were like them that dream.

> Then was our mouth filled with laughter,
> and our tongue with singing. . . .
>
> (KJV)

When I read those words, "Then was our mouth filled with laughter," my mind instantly went back to my experience the previous night when that river of laughter had flowed out through me. I could attest the accuracy of the description. It did not say, "we laughed"; it said, "our mouth [was] filled with laughter." It was as though the laughter came from another source, filled them, and flowed out through their mouths. That was exactly what had happened to me.

I must confess, my reaction was, "How could I go to church all those years and no one ever tell me that this is in the Bible?"

As I continued to read the Bible, again and again I found that the things which happened in my life through the Holy Spirit were described in the Bible. In fact, I found that there was no other place to which I could go for a meaningful explanation of what was happening in my life.

In most cases, from that day until this, when I begin to read the Bible it is as if there are just two persons in the universe, God and me — and the Bible is God speaking to me.

Since I got to know the Author, I have never had a theological or an intellectual problem believing the Bible is the Word of God. As a matter of fact, I do not feel in any way intellectually inferior to people who do not believe the Bible. I was a professional logician and excelled in that particular field, and, on the basis of my own examination, the Bible is the most intellectually sound and logical book I have ever read. It is the Word of God, a personal God speaking to me with a living voice, as a person.

Let me now relate two other objective results of my meeting with Jesus. The first one is rather comical, but it is very real. The next evening, after I had this encounter with Jesus, I went to the pub to get my usual quota of whiskey. I had no moral or religious scruples about drinking whiskey. When I got to the door of the pub, intending to walk in, the most extraordinary thing happened—my legs locked! And no matter how hard I tried, I could not get them to carry my body into that pub! At first, I felt indignant and frustrated. I realized I no longer was interested in what that place had to offer. I no longer needed whiskey to relax. I had found something that was deep and permanent, and its effects were far more enduring than those of whiskey. So I just turned around and walked out.

The final result I will express in the words of Jesus in John 7:37–39:

> Now on the last day, the great day of the feast, Jesus stood and cried out, saying, "If any man is thirsty, let him come to Me and drink. He who believes in Me, as the Scripture said, 'From his innermost being shall flow rivers of living water.' " But this He spoke of the Spirit, whom those who believed in Him were to receive; for the Spirit was not yet given, because Jesus was not yet glorified.   (NAS)

Let me target those words, "If any man is thirsty." Looking back, I realized that I had been a thirsty man for many years, but I did not know where to quench my thirst. The Bible reveals that man is made up of three elements: spirit, soul and body. The predominant feature of Plato's teaching is his emphasis on the soul. I had sought satisfaction for my soul in many different ways: in philosophy, in music, in art, in travel. I had sought satisfaction for my body in many ways. When I sought all those satisfactions, I remained unsatisfied.

As a result of this experience, I realized that the part of me that was thirsty was not my soul nor my body, but my spirit. When the Holy Spirit came in, He instantly supplied the satisfaction for that thirst. I became just like Jesus said: a channel for rivers of water.

PART II

DISCIPLED IN THE DESERT

6
MANNA IN THE DESERT

Very soon after I had come to know Jesus in this real and personal way, my company was sent to North Africa, and I spent the next three years in the deserts of Egypt, Libya and the Sudan. It is interesting to trace in the Bible how God sometimes used the desert to prepare His people for their future service. There are some vivid descriptions of deserts in the Bible. For example, Jeremiah 2:6:

> "They did not ask, 'Where is the LORD,
>   who brought us up out of Egypt
> and led us through the barren wilderness,
>   through a land of deserts and rifts,
> a land of drought and darkness,
>   a land where no one travels and no one
>   lives?' " (NIV)

In the desert, I once read that verse to my fellow soldiers and they all agreed that it was an exact description of the situation in which we found ourselves.

The desert strips the non-essentials from us and brings us down to the basics of life. In the material realm there are four basics. Stated in order of importance they are water, food, shelter, and transportation.

In the spiritual realm also, my years in the desert stripped away many non-essentials and brought me down to the spiritual basics. When I think back to that time, I am reminded of how Moses described God's dealings with Israel when He led them through the desert. Deuteronomy 32:10:

> He [the Lord] found him in a desert land,
> and in the waste howling wilderness; he led
> him about, he instructed him, he kept him
> as the apple of his eye.
>
> (KJV)

Moses describes four successive stages, all of which were fulfilled in my experience: first, the Lord *found*; second, He *led*; third, He *instructed*; and fourth, He *kept*. There is a logical order here. As we are willing to be led by Him, He instructs us. Then, as we are willing to be instructed, He keeps us. But His keeping us depends on our being led and instructed! Read those words again. They are so vivid.

In the desert, one thing especially that God revealed to Israel was the real source of nourishment and life. In Deuteronomy 8:2–3, Moses reminds Israel of their experience during the forty years in the wilderness:

> "And you shall remember all the way which
> the LORD your God has led you in the

wilderness these forty years, that He might humble you, testing you, to know what was in your heart, whether you would keep His commandments or not. And He humbled you and let you be hungry, and fed you with manna which you did not know, nor did your fathers know, that He might make you understand that man does not live by bread alone, but man lives by everything that proceeds out of the mouth of the LORD."

(NAS)

The real source of life is not just physical material bread, it is that which proceeds out of the mouth of the Lord! Another translation reads, ". . . the word that comes out of the mouth of the Lord." The real life source is God and His Word. In order that Israel might learn this, God humbled them, tested them, and, in particular, allowed them to be hungry.

I can tell you from experience, when you are in the desert, being hungry is a test! There were many days we did not have enough to eat and had only brackish water to drink, and very little of that.

I was in charge of a group of eight men who were called "stretcher bearers," though they did very little stretcher bearing. There were also two drivers who shared the driving of the big three-ton truck in which we traveled through the desert. All together, there were ten men and myself on that truck. Before very long, the rest of our company had dubbed us "Prince's Pioneers" because I was the one in charge of this motley group.

Being hungry brings out things in you of which you are

unaware. Many times it was a test of unselfishness and discipline whether we would be content with our rations or would try to cheat in order to get some rations that belonged to another man. It really was a humbling experience, but in it all God showed me that He had made provision for my spiritual life through the Bible and through the Holy Spirit. The Bible was my manna! I lived on it day by day.

Job said, "I have esteemed the words of his mouth more than my necessary food" (Job 23:12 KJV). I could honestly say that was true of me. If I had to choose between eating or reading the Bible, I chose reading the Bible. I was living by the words that proceeded out of the mouth of God there in that desert.

In 1 Corinthians 10, Paul brings out some of the lessons that God taught Israel during the years in the wilderness, and reminded the Christians to whom He was writing that those lessons had an application for them as well. First Corinthians 10:1–4 says:

> For I do not want you to be unaware, brethren, that our fathers were all under the cloud, and all passed through the sea ["our fathers" means Israel]; and all were baptized into Moses in the cloud and in the sea; and all ate the same spiritual food; and all drank the same spiritual drink, for they were drinking from a spiritual rock which followed them; and the rock was Christ.
>
> (NAS)

There were four experiences appointed for all of God's people. The first two experiences were single events: two baptisms, or immersions. All God's people were baptized into Moses, their leader; that is, they were set apart to Moses as their leader by a double baptism: first, the baptism in the cloud (which corresponds to the baptism in the Holy Spirit for us as Christians); and, second, the baptism in the sea (which corresponds to water baptism). Those two baptisms set Israel apart to Moses their leader. Our two baptisms (in water and in the Holy Spirit), set us apart to Jesus Christ as our leader.

After that, there were two ongoing daily experiences for Israel in the wilderness: first, the manna (which God provided supernaturally from heaven); and, second, the water from the rock. Paul tells us that the rock was Christ, the Messiah. They therefore had a double source of spiritual nourishment: the manna, which corresponds to God's Word; and the water, which corresponds to the Holy Spirit.

So it was in my period in the desert. I lived by the Word and by the Spirit. In three years in the desert, I gained a basic knowledge of the Bible. I read it through a number of times and I discovered that the interpreter of Scripture is the Holy Spirit. In God's marvelous provision for us, the Holy Spirit, who is the author of Scripture, also becomes our teacher and our interpreter. I soon discovered that whenever I needed to know anything that was practical and relevant to my spiritual life, the Holy Spirit would always lead me to the answer in the Scriptures. When I started attending church some years later, I discovered that there was much more in the Bible than we hear about in most churches. I was often disappointed at how little the churches told us of the Bible. I soon learned to judge the church by the Bible, and not the Bible by the church.

7
CRUCIFIED AND
BURIED WITH CHRIST

God sometimes uses the desert to prepare His people for their future service. The desert strips away from us the non-essentials and brings us down to the basics of life.

In the desert, we traveled almost incessantly on a three-ton truck. Desert warfare is extremely mobile. On this truck I traveled with eight men called "stretcher bearers" and two men who were responsible for driving and maintaining the truck. I was in charge of the total group. The rest of our company had dubbed us "Prince's Pioneers." We had a little flag bearing that title that we would put up each time we stopped for the night.

We usually slept out in the open desert which, although it was usually hot in the daytime, became cold very quickly at night. Sand gathers heat very quickly, but also loses it very quickly. There was an art in learning where to sleep and how to keep warm. I usually used my boots as a pillow and one of the wheels of the truck as a shelter from the wind.

We were each allotted four blankets. When I look back,

it is almost comical how important those blankets were to us. Today I would not think much about four coarse blankets, but I had one particular blanket which really was my most cherished material possession. I think it must have been a horse blanket originally because it was at least twice as large as any normal blanket, but it only counted as one. So I had three blankets, plus a great, huge horse blanket.

I learned how to stretch them out on the sand, putting some under me and some over me, and to sleep in such a way that I was almost shut off from the wind and the cold. So I had a little nightly home there inside my four blankets.

As a new believer, there were many things about spiritual life I did not understand, so I was continually questioning and arguing with God. I wanted to know why we had to go on like this day after day, and what good it was doing. Why couldn't God get me out of the army? He knew that I wanted to serve Him. I had a lot of questions and complaints, and I was far from being restful at times.

Because we had no artificial light, we usually went to sleep just about the time the sun set and got up when the sun rose. One night I wrapped myself in my blankets and lay down there on the sand. As I lay there arguing with God, I found myself pinned down on my back (I believe it must have been by the power of the Holy Spirit), with the blankets wrapped about me in a strange way so that I could not move. My arms were stretched out horizontally from my body, with my palms upwards. In some strange way, I could not get into another position. It was as though I was pinned down by those blankets. Suddenly, I realized I was in the exact position of a person being crucified on a cross. The next day, when I opened up the Bible, my eyes fell on Galatians 2:20 where Paul says:

"I have been crucified with Christ and I no longer live, but Christ lives in me. The life I live in the body, I live by faith in the Son of God, who loved me and gave himself for me."

(NIV)

In that very vivid way, without my reasoning it out, the Holy Spirit showed me that in God's sight I was crucified with Christ. Thus, I had nothing to argue about, no case to plead: I was a crucified person! Christ's crucifixion had become my crucifixion. He had identified Himself with me and my sin in His death on the cross. Now I must identify myself with Him and see myself as crucified with Him. The crucified man has nothing to argue about and no case to plead; he is just there. He takes his position and is held there because that is the position that has been ordained for him.

In that demonstration of the power of the Holy Spirit working through those blankets that pinned me down on my back, I learned to say, "I have been crucified with Christ. That is my position. That is my condition. Now I don't live. I have no arguments, or pleas, or claims. I have no rights. Those have been stripped from me by crucifixion. I am to see myself as a crucified person. That is how God sees me."

Another night, a little later, I had a somewhat similar experience. I was again wrapped up in my blankets, with my head against the wheel of the truck trying to keep out the biting cold wind. Again I found myself pinned, but I was in a different position. I was on my back, but my hands were pinned down by my side. Struggle as I would, I could not get free. There was a mysterious power operating through those blankets that bound me in that position.

As I ceased struggling and just lay there, I realized I was in the position of a man being carried out for burial. I realized that not only was I crucified with Christ, but I was also buried with Christ. While a person is being crucified, they are still visible, but when a person is buried, they have been put out of sight and are no longer visible. There is no longer any evidence of their life. Again I turned to the New Testament and read that that is how God sees me. Colossians 2:12:

> . . . having been buried with him in baptism
> and raised with him through your faith in
> the power of God, who raised him from the
> dead.   (NIV)

I saw that I was buried with Christ and that only through burial could I enter into the resurrection life that God had for me. First I must be crucified, then buried, and then I could be resurrected. I noticed that it said "buried with him in baptism," and that lodged in my mind and started a train of thought.

Nearly a year later, in 1942, after I had been in the desert and had not seen a paved road in nine or ten months, the army gave me a brief leave and permitted me to go to Jerusalem for the first time. Going to Jerusalem from the desert sand was really like going to heaven from hell. The first time I saw Jerusalem, I fell in love with her and must testify now that I have been in love with her ever since.

While in Jerusalem, I was introduced to a Christian minister who explained to me the spiritual and scriptural basis of water baptism. God gave me the wonderful privilege one day in August 1942 of being immersed in the waters of the Jordan (baptized) on the basis of my faith in Jesus as my Savior, probably not more than a quarter of a mile from the place where Jesus Himself had been baptized by John the Baptist.

When I was actually buried with Christ by baptism, I discovered that it produced some important changes. I experienced a wonderful deliverance from my old way of life. Many of the old pictures, scenes and incidents which remained in my mind had come back to trouble me. After I had been baptized in the Jordan, I realized that those pictures, scenes and memories from the past had been erased. They were no longer there to trouble, curse or torment me. I saw that it is important, not merely to be dead, but to be buried. It is not enough that we have a dead body, but, in order for that body to be dealt with in the proper way, it must be baptized, or buried. God taught me that lesson there in the wilderness and then in the River Jordan.

8

THE DISCIPLINE
OF FASTING

God taught me two further practical lessons during this period. The first relates to fasting. Let me give a brief definition of fasting. Fasting is abstaining from food, deliberately, for spiritual purposes. In most cases in the Bible where people fasted, they abstained from food, but not from water. Sometimes they also abstained from water, but that was an exception.

One of the things that the Holy Spirit showed me immediately (maybe only four weeks after I had come to know the Lord), is that fasting is a normal part of Christian life and discipline. It is not something strange or "way out" that only a few fanatics sometimes practice. It is a normal part of Christian life and discipline. Later on, when I was able to attend church and hear preaching, I was astonished that so many Christians seemed to know nothing whatever about fasting. The Bible is full of fasting, even in the New Testament.

Jesus Himself fasted and assumed that His disciples

would fast. In the Sermon on the Mount, when Jesus laid down the principles of the Christian life in Matthew 6, He said to them, "When you fast." In other words, He assumed that they would be fasting and gave them the principles to follow. In chapter six He said "when" about three things: *when* you give alms, *when* you pray, and *when* you fast. He assumed that all His disciples would do all three of those things: give alms, pray and fast.

If we look on in the New Testament, we find that the early church fasted corporately and that its leaders fasted. Paul said of himself that he was "often in fastings." It was something he practiced frequently.

In the Old Testament, you will find that many of God's most faithful servants fasted. To name just a few: Moses, David, Elijah, Ezra, Nehemiah and Esther. You will find that in some cases the fasting of God's people brought down divine intervention and changed the course of history.

Without my knowing all these facts from the Bible, the Holy Spirit showed me that God wanted me to fast. So in the desert for two or three years, I normally fasted each Wednesday by going without food. The reaction of my fellow soldiers was somewhat amusing. The Moslems have one month in the year, Ramadan, where they do not eat in the daytime. They eat plenty at night, but nothing in the daytime. Because we were in Egypt, a Moslem country, the British soldiers had learned a little about Ramadan. The soldiers in my particular company used to call Wednesday "Ramadan" because that was the day I fasted. Of course, I did not make a show of fasting, but when you are living in close quarters every hour of the day and night, not eating meals will certainly be noticed.

The attitude of my fellow soldiers was rather remarkable.

After they saw that my faith was genuine and that I was really leading a life that corresponded to what I believed (although they did not want to join me in my faith), they respected me. In a strange way they were glad to have me because in moments of danger they considered me to be a kind of insurance policy. In one case, our little medical unit was cut off behind enemy lines and we did not know where we were going to end up. One of those tough, blaspheming British soldiers said to me, "Corporal Prince, I'm glad you're here with us." So, although they did not follow my example, they respected my life, and I think I was a kind of help and protection to those soldiers. For two years of active service we hardly lost one man out of that company, which was a very unusual record in those circumstances.

Interestingly enough, later when I read the journal of John Wesley, the founder of the Methodists, I discovered that he practiced fasting regularly, and that he would not ordain a man to the Methodist ministry who would not promise to fast each Wednesday and Friday until 4 p.m. God had shown this lesson to others, but He showed it to me also, individually and personally.

This is one specific example of how God answered prayer for me when I fasted. Desert conditions tend to provoke murmuring or complaining, which is very obvious in the history of the children of Israel. It happened many times with Israel and brought God's judgment and disfavor upon them for which they had to repent. I went through some of the same experiences. I began to complain. I got so weary of the desert and the food and the blaspheming British soldiers that I said, "Lord, why do you keep me here? Why can't you give me some other place to be?"

When I did this, I lost my sense of God's presence and

blessing. I knew that God still cared for me and was real, but my close, intimate, personal relationship with God that had become so precious to me seemed to have disappeared.

One day I decided to set aside a special day (not a Wednesday), to fast and ask God the reason why His presence seemed to have been withdrawn from me. I spent the whole day fasting. I asked, "God, why aren't you near to me? Why must I continue in this monotonous, wearisome life in this desert?"

By the evening, God had given me an answer. He spoke very clearly in words that I can record for you. He said, "Why have you not thanked Me? Why have you not praised Me?"

As I meditated on what God said, I began to see that I had become unthankful and that I had stopped thanking God and praising Him. That was why I had lost the sense of His presence.

In that way I learned the importance of continual thanksgiving and praise in the Christian life. The Holy Spirit then directed me to various Scriptures along this line. One of those Scriptures is 1 Thessalonians 5:16–19:

> Rejoice always [even in the desert]; pray without ceasing; in everything give thanks [and "everything" includes being there in the desert with the flies and the sand and the bad food and the blaspheming soldiers]; for this is God's will for you in Christ Jesus. Do not quench the Spirit. . . .
>
> (NAS)

The implication is that if we do not always rejoice, if we

do not pray without ceasing, and if we do not give thanks in everything, we are quenching the Holy Spirit! That is just what I had done by murmuring and complaining. Instead of praising and giving thanks, I had quenched the Holy Spirit in my life.

The second passage is in Hebrews 13:15:

> Through Him then, let us continually offer
> up a sacrifice of praise to God, that is, the
> fruit of lips that give thanks to His name.
>
> (NAS)

There again I saw that God expects us to continually offer up a sacrifice of praise which comes from our lips, not just inwardly from our hearts. We must make our praise vocal by giving thanks to the name of the Lord!

I also saw that praise is a sacrifice. This was a real lesson for me. Sacrifice costs something. I must praise God the most when I feel like praising Him the least because my praise was most acceptable to God at that time. I adjusted my life and I learned the discipline of giving thanks and praising God in every situation and circumstance. Do you know what I discovered? My circumstances did not change, but I did! When I changed, then my view of my circumstances become different, too.

9
ONE YEAR
IN HOSPITAL

For almost three years while I served as a hospital attendant with the British Forces in the deserts of North Africa, I had no opportunity to attend a church or listen to a preacher. In a very real sense, God Himself discipled me in three main ways: through the Bible, through the Holy Spirit, and through the successive situations and circumstances in which I found myself. Looking back, I see how God systematically arranged one situation after another in order to teach me the great basic principles that I would need in my subsequent service for Him. When I think about this, I am always reminded of what Moses said about God's dealings with Jacob in Deuteronomy 32:10:

> He found him in a desert land, and in the waste howling wilderness; he led him about, he instructed him, he kept him as the apple of his eye.
>
> (KJV)

God found him, He led him, He instructed him, and He kept him. That is the order in which God deals with us. First, He *finds* us, then He *leads* us. If we are willing to be led, He *instructs* us. Then, if we are willing to be instructed, He *keeps* us. Being instructed, however, depends upon being led; and being kept depends upon being led and instructed. That was the order in my life, as well. God found me; He led me; He instructed me; and I thank God, He kept me. Through one year that I spent in the hospital as a patient I learned vital lessons.

I was part of a medical unit that was to provide medical services to the troops of an armored division in North Africa. We went together through the Battle of El Alamein, the great turning point of the war in North Africa. We shared in that victory and began the move westward across the Egyptian desert into Libya. As I was moving with my company, I became sick with a condition that was undoubtedly due to the desert, the food, and possibly also to my emotional reaction to these things. The skin on my feet, and later my hands, became raw, sore and infected. After awhile I could not wear army boots and then found it difficult to walk. The medical officer I worked with valued my services and did everything he could to keep me out of the hospital, but eventually he had to say, "There's no alternative. I'll have to let you go into the hospital."

So I was admitted into a hospital in Libya and later transferred to two successive hospitals in Egypt. All together, I spent almost exactly one year in British military hospitals in North Africa. Much of the time I was a bed patient. My condition would clear up temporarily, but the moment I began to use my feet or expose myself to the sun or sand, the condition reopened. It was a comparatively common condition with British soldiers in North Africa.

I remember being in one ward with a British soldier who had been in the Middle East two years and had spent eighteen months in a hospital with that condition. Apparently, in that location and with the facilities available to them at the time, the doctors really did not have a satisfactory medical answer. They gave my condition various long names, each doctor picking a new one. Eventually, it was characterized as chronic eczema, but whatever name was given to it, the medical profession in that location did not have a complete cure.

As I lay there during that one year, there were many, many battles going on in my mind. I had two main enemies that assailed my mind, both of which began with "d." One was doubt and the other was depression. I was a believer, knew the Lord and was committed to Him, yet I lay there having these raging battles in my mind against doubt and depression. "Had God forgotten about me? Did He really care for me? Could He heal me? What was going to happen to me?"

One of the things I said over and over again was, "I know that if I had faith, God would heal me."

But the next thing I always said was, ". . . but I know I don't have faith."

Every time I said, "I don't have faith," I was right there in that dark, lonely Valley of Despair. God sent help to me through His Word by one particular verse of Scripture, Romans 10:17. "So then faith cometh by hearing, and hearing by the word of God" (KJV).

I laid hold of two words: "faith cometh." They were like a ray of light in the darkness of that lonely valley. Faith comes! If you don't have it, you can get it.

How does it come? I studied that verse over and over. "Faith comes by hearing." Hearing what? God's Word. If I wanted faith, I could get it—if I could hear God's Word.

I knew God's Word was there in my hand; in the Bible that I held before me. How could I get faith? By hearing what God was saying to me by His Holy Spirit through His Word. I determined that was what I would do.

I determined I was going to hear what God was saying to me, that I was going to try to shut out other voices, and not listen to doubt or depression when they attacked my mind. From then on, I determined to focus my entire attention on what God was saying to me in His Word.

I thought of a practical way to do this. I armed myself with a blue pencil and decided I would read through the entire Bible and underline in blue four related themes: healing, health, physical strength, and long life. It took me about four months to get through the Bible. But when I had finished and looked back through it, I had a blue Bible! There was hardly a page anywhere in the Bible where I had not used my blue pencil.

Interestingly enough, there were probably two books that contained the most blue pencil marks. One was in the Old Testament, Proverbs; and the other was in the New Testament, Matthew. But the whole Bible was filled with passages underlined in blue. I realized that healing is one of the major messages of the Bible, and that God is a Healer! I saw, time and time again, how God revealed Himself to His people. Exodus 15:26: "I am the Lord that healeth thee" (KJV) or "I, the Lord, am your healer" (NAS).

Continually, God said to His people, "If you will obey Me, if you will keep My covenant and My statutes, I will put none of these evil diseases upon you. I am the Lord that healeth thee."

Psalm 103:2–3: "Bless the LORD, O my soul, and forget not all his benefits: who forgiveth all thine iniquities; who healeth all thy diseases" (KJV).

Matthew 8:17: "He Himself took our infirmities and bore our sicknesses (NKJ)."

I discovered that Jesus spent many hours ministering to the sick, probably more time than He spent preaching. As I completed this study, my whole image of God underwent a radical change. I had grown up with a kind of boyish image of God (if I can say this reverently) as a rather irritable old man with a long beard, who lived a long way off in an office somewhere. If you were in trouble, you were required to go to His office. I pictured Him as a grumpy, unreasonable school master.

Now, however, through hearing what God was saying to me through the Bible and focusing my attention on it, my picture of God changed. I saw God as a loving Father. I saw Him as one who planned the best. I saw that if I could commit my life to Him without reservation, He would arrange everything for the best. He loved me, He cared for me, He had made provision for me and wanted the best for me. My whole religious background fell away from me.

I had always had the impression that if you were going to be a Christian, you must prepare to be miserable. I think it went back to those words I heard so many times in the Anglican Church service, "Pardon us, miserable offenders." Somehow, it made a deep impact on me that Christians were miserable people and that God was a harsh, stern, unreasonable God. That image changed and I saw God as loving and wise, gracious and kind, and able to provide for His people and to keep them in every situation and circumstance.

10
GOD'S MEDICINE BOTTLE

Healing is one of the main themes of the Bible and one of the main provisions of God for His people. Now I began to see God as a loving Father, one who cares for His children and makes every possible provision for them, who always wants the best and is able to provide it. The second part of this story is that after faith had come, it led me to healing.

As I continued studying the Bible and seeking the truth about healing, I had one particular mental problem from my background in philosophy. It was hard for me to accept statements in their plain, straightforward meaning. When I remember that we spent one whole term discussing whether the desk from which the philosophy professor spoke was really there, I can see how philosophy had trained me to doubt even the simplest things.

This was a mental problem that still troubled me, even while I was reading the Bible and underlining in blue. It seemed to me that there were some things that were so simple they could not possibly mean what they said, especially about physical healing. I still had a residue of what I would call a "religious view," that the body is unimportant and that God does not care much about it. God cares about the soul, which is going to go to heaven and be with Him, but the body is corruptible, and will one day die. God could not really be too concerned, in the meanwhile, whether our body was well or sick. Or could He?

Now there are many, many statements in the Bible that contradict that, but I found it hard to take them at their face value. For instance, in Psalm 103:2, David says:

> Bless the LORD, O my soul, and forget not
> all his benefits:
> Who forgiveth all thine iniquities; who
> healeth all thy diseases.
>
> (KJV)

That was so clear, but my philosophic mind said, "But that's only diseases of the soul. That does not mean physical diseases; that means mental and emotional diseases."

Subsequently, I have studied the Bible in the original language and I saw that is an impossible way of representing the meaning of the Hebrew word for "soul." But at that time it was a real problem for me. I said, "Certainly, God heals, but He's really interested in spiritual healing. He's not much interested in our physical bodies."

Then one day the Holy Spirit directed me to Proverbs 4:20–22. This is the passage that got me out of the hospital. I want to emphasize the importance of being directed by the Holy Spirit. He is the One who directs us to that particular portion of the Word that represents what we need to give us the faith that we need at any given moment. In Proverbs 4:20–22, God says to His children who know Him personally:

> My son, attend to my words; incline thine ear unto my sayings.
> Let them not depart from thine eyes; keep them in the midst of thine heart.
> For they are life unto those that find them, and health to all their flesh.
>
> (KJV)

When I got to those last words, "health to all their flesh," I said to myself, "That settles it! Not even a philosopher can make 'flesh' mean 'spirit.'" Flesh is flesh, my physical body, and God says He has provided health for all my physical body.

My philosophy helped me here because I thought, "Logically, if I can have health in all my physical body, there can be no room for sickness anywhere. Sickness and health are opposites. Where there is sickness, there is no health. Where there is health, there is no sickness."

I looked in the margin of the Bible I was using and the alternative reading for "health" was "medicine." So I saw that God had provided "medicine," which He guaranteed would give me health in my whole physical body. I determined to take God's Word as my medicine. God said it was His words and His sayings that would be health, or medicine, to all my flesh.

I was a hospital attendant and one of my jobs had been to give people medicine. Again, I decided to be simple and down-to-earth. I wondered, "How do people take medicine?" In those days it was three times daily, after meals. So I reasoned, "That's what I'm going to do. I'm going to take God's Word as my medicine three times daily, after meals."

As I decided to take God's Word as my medicine, God spoke very clearly to my mind. He said, "When the doctor gives you medicine, the directions for taking it are on the bottle. If you want Me to be your doctor, this is My medicine bottle, and the directions for taking it are on the bottle. You'd better read them."

So I looked back at the passage and I saw that there were four clear directions for taking God's Word as my medicine.

First, "attend to My words." I must give very careful, undivided attention to what God was saying. This was in line with what I had already seen about how faith comes.

Second, "incline thine ear unto My sayings." I realized that inclining or bowing down my ear meant bowing down my whole head. You cannot bow down your ear without bowing down your head. Bowing down my head meant to take a respectful, reverent, humble and teachable attitude toward God. Again, as I read God's Word about His goodness and His willingness to heal and provide, I thought, "That's too good to be true! I really could not be understanding it right."

After I had done that many times, the Lord said to me, "Who is the teacher and who is the pupil?"

I thought it over and said, "Lord, you are the teacher and I am the pupil."

The Lord replied, "Well, would you mind letting Me teach?"

Then I realized what it meant to "incline your ear." It meant to stop arguing, to stop telling God what He ought to have said and to believe what He was saying. I was like many other people. I approached the Bible with my mind made up in advance, through tradition and background, as to what God ought to have said. If God actually said something different from what I thought, it was very difficult for me to hear Him at all. So the second instruction is to incline your ear, bow down, and be humble. Do not argue with God but be teachable, let Him tell you.

Third, "let them not depart from thine eyes." I saw that I must keep my eyes focused on the promises of God. If my eyes strayed from God's promises to other kinds of suggestions or teachings that were not in line with the Word of God, then I did not receive the healing effect of God's Word in my body.

Fourth, "keep them in the midst of thine heart." I saw how true that is psychologically. God uses the "eye gate" and the "ear gate." He says, in effect, "Incline your ears and focus your eyes. In that way, through the ear gate and the eye gate combined, My Word will come into your heart and when it is in your heart, it will provide healing and health for all your flesh."

The very next verse says, "Keep thy heart with all diligence, for out of it are the issues of life." That is very true. What you get into your heart is going to determine the issues of your life.

So I took God's Word faithfully as my medicine, three times daily after meals, for about three or four months. As a result, I received a complete and permanent healing. I have walked in that health for nearly forty years from that day until now. So God's Word is true! You can trust it! He does provide health to all our flesh!

As I look back now on that situation in which I found

myself, I see that I was at a crossroads in my life. I was confronted with the clear truth of God's Word, but as a philosopher I found it difficult to believe it so simply. I realized that I had only two alternatives:

One, I could go on making things complicated and stay sick; or, two, I could be willing to make things simple and get well.

Looking back, I am so glad that I was willing to make things simple and get well. Let me offer that advice to you: Make things simple. Believe God's Word and get well.

God bless you.

ABOUT THE AUTHOR

Derek Prince (1915–2003) was born in India of British parents. Educated as a scholar of Greek and Latin at Eton College and Cambridge University, England, he held a Fellowship in Ancient and Modern Philosophy at King's College. He also studied several modern languages, including Hebrew and Aramaic, at Cambridge University and the Hebrew University in Jerusalem.

While serving with the British army in World War II, he began to study the Bible and experienced a life-changing encounter with Jesus Christ. Out of this encounter he formed two conclusions: first, that Jesus Christ is alive; second, that the Bible is a true, relevant, up-to-date book. These conclusions altered the whole course of his life, which he then devoted to studying and teaching the Bible.

Derek's main gift of explaining the Bible and its teaching in a clear and simple way has helped build a foundation of faith in millions of lives. His non-denominational, non-sectarian approach has made his teaching equally relevant and helpful to people from all racial and religious backgrounds.

He is the author of over 50 books, 500 audio and 160 video teaching cassettes, many of which have been translated and published in more than 60 languages. His daily radio broadcast, Keys to Successful Living, is translated into Arabic, Chinese (Amoy, Cantonese, Mandarin, Shanghaiese, Swatow), Croatian, German, Malagasy, Mongolian, Russian, Samoan, Spanish and Tongan. His daily radio program continues to touch lives around the world.